MESSAGE TO THE YOUNG KINGS AND QUEENS

You are the FUTURE and the NOW! Understand that you can be as successful as you want to be in life but reaching your full potential will depend on the decisions you make now and the effort you give consistently moving forward. Never jeopardize the opportunity to reach your full potential by limiting your expectations. Also, understand that adversity is going to happen. You may encounter a professor you don't understand. You may have transportation issues. A family member could get sick. It is inevitable.

Everything is not going to work in your favor every step of the way. The real test of your character is how you respond when adversity happens. Nothing will come to you in your comfort zone, but once you understand that adversity builds character, you will also recognize that the adversity you endure is your POWER. As you navigate through this book, I want you to think about the bigger picture. Always go deeper. If you desire greatness, greatness is upon you. To achieve greatness, be willing to have faith, do work, make sacrifices, and much more. You have what it takes. Let's make the TRANSITION!

Blake "Professor B" Simon

THE COLLEGE MASTER ACTION PLAN

THE TRANSITION
GUIDE & JOURNAL

A SIMPLE TOOL FOR STUDENTS TO HELP MAXIMIZE THE COLLEGE EXPERIENCE

THIRD EDITION

D. BLAKE SIMON
Prairie View A&M University

Co-Author

_____

Your Name

BLAKE SIMON & ASSOCIATES

© 2019 D. Blake Simon

Disclaimer: The information published in this book represents the opinions, personal research, and professional experience of the author. The author makes no guarantees and disclaims any personal loss or liabilities that may occur as a result of the use of information herein. If legal advice or other expert assistance is required, the services of a competent professional person should be sought.

Further, you should be aware that internet websites listed in this book may have changed or disappeared between when this book was written and when it is read.

Special discounts are available on quantity purchases by organizations, corporations, and other groups or businesses. To book the author for your event or other business inquiries, visit **www.blakemotivates.com/booking**

Independently published
Cover photo: shot by Mark Landry at Southern A&M University, 2018 marklandry04@gmail.com
Back cover photo: by ShotbyArthur (@Shotbyarthur)
Concept contributor: Alton Russell, Higher Education Professional

ISBN: 9781798768808

Blake Simon & Associates (BSA)
www.BlakeMotivates.com

ABOUT THE AUTHOR

BLAKE "PROFESSOR B" SIMON
Speaker · Author · Professor · Influencer

Based on his unique life experiences as a student and professional, Blake "Professor B" Simon developed a passion for preparing students and families for post-secondary success. After spending four years in higher education as a financial aid counselor working closely with students and families, he moved on to pursue his passion full-time.

Professor B created "The Transition" platform which has impacted thousands of students and families across the nation through transparent talks, thought-provoking sessions, and practical curriculums focused on cognitive development, life skills, and first-year experience. He has authored "The Transition" book series including *The Transition Guide & Journal: A Simple Tool for Students to Help Maximize the College Experience*, which is a student game changer! Blake later returned to higher education as an Adjunct Professor at Houston Community College. As an alumnus of Prairie View A&M University, Blake understands the opportunity that comes along with education but is not naïve to the obstacles facing our youth. He continues to use his platform to fight for education equality in his community and across the country!

DEDICATION

To the memory of
Virgie "Feesee" Harrison, who raised me and
taught me to be caring, passionate, and
determined,

With love to my sister, Mia Mouton and my family,

and to the Underdog student, keep your head high
and never give up

Rest in Peace Drew Conley
Remember 3

CONTENTS

TRANSITION

TRAN·SI·TION | \TRAN(T)-ˈSI-SHƏN

NOUN

1. passage from state, stage, subject, or place to another

2. a movement, development, or evolution from one form, state, or style to another

INTRANSITIVE VERB

1. to make a change from one state, place, or condition to another: to make a Transtion

FAITH IS TAKING

THE FIRST

STEP EVEN

{ WHEN YOU }

CAN'T SEE

THE WHOLE

STAIRCASE

-MARTIN LUTHER KING JR.

INTRODUCTION

THE TRANSITION COLLEGE MAP

"Education is the most powerful weapon which you can use to change the world." --Nelson Mandela

The Transition Guide & Journal: A Simple Tool for Students to Help Maximize the College Experience 3rd Edition is created from the ground up with a practical approach to student success in college. This guidebook will empower students to become active learners whose mindsets will shift to meet any challenge presented while making the "Transition" to college, through college, and beyond. The Transition Guide & Journal can be used as a primary or supplemental resource for First Year Experience (FYE) or Student Success courses and initiatives. Moreover, students and families can find in this book a wealth of practical information and action steps to help guide their transition.

PURPOSE

Pursuing higher education is a decision that should be taken seriously. Students are always pushed to "go to college," but rarely are they given a plan on how to be successful while making that transition. This resource provides a guideline for students on how to create a plan and execute it effectively while transitioning to and through college.

OVERVIEW

What will you discover as you work through this guidebook? *The Transition Guide & Journal: A Simple Tool for Students to Help Maximize the College Experience 3rd Edition* is divided into three sections and introduces the College **M**aster **A**ction **P**lan (MAP).

Section I: The Foundation Plan

This section focuses on developing a winning mindset and laying a solid foundation. The Foundation Plan consists of the 5 Foundation Keys. These keys focus on purpose, goal setting, affirmations, preparation, and trusting the process.

Chapter 1: The Why
Chapter 2: A Different You
Chapter 3: The Formula to Success
Chapter 4: Create Your Own Luck
Chapter 5: Trust the Process

Section II: The Academic Plan

This section focuses on developing the tools to be successful academically in the higher education environment. Some of the topics covered in this section include selecting a career and major, maximizing campus resources, building effective relationships and networking, and time management.

Chapter 6: College & Beyond

Chapter 7: Key Campus Resources

Chapter 8: Networking& Relationships

Chapter 9: Time Management

Section III: The Financial Plan

This section focuses on building an effective financial plan for success in college through financial aid literacy and budgeting basics.

Chapter 10: Understanding Financial Aid

Cheater 11: Budgeting Basics

Throughout the text, I also share personal experiences related to my transition to college, through college, and beyond. Each section has interactive exercises designed to help students maximize the information provided throughout the text.

EXERCISES

Each section also has interactive exercises designed to help students maximize the information provided throughout the text.

Section I: The Foundation Plan

Exercise 1: What's Your Why

Exercise 2: Positive Affirmations

Exercise 3: 10 M.A.P. Goals

Section II: The Academic Plan

Exercise 4: Plan Your Next Two Semesters

Exercise 5: Locate the Resource

Exercise 6: 10 People to know on Campus

Section III: The Financial Plan

Exercise 7: Determine Your Financial Aid Status

THE TRANSITION DEGREE

Once the student completes their reading of the text and the exercises, they receive the Transition Degree in The Law of Attraction! The purpose of the Transition degree is to encourage a student to complete the degree he or she is seeking.

THE JOURNAL

Writing is a game-changing tool that can alter your life for the best. Some people avoid the idea of writing, but personally, some of my greatest achievements have started with an idea, a pen, and paper. I've also used writing as an outlet to help me overcome adversities throughout my life.

You may get frustrated at your peers, professors, and even family members. Instead of taking to social media or expressing your feelings ways that may come back to haunt you, journaling is a great way to channel those emotions and turn them into something constructive.

Writing and journaling will also create an opportunity to record your goals, experiences, thoughts, and essential lessons or occurrences from your day. Simply put, writing is powerful if you allow it to be. As a result, at the end of each section, there will be journal space available to for you to write and journal your way through the transition. Use the journal areas as YOUR creative space!

"Writing in a journal reminds you of your goals and of your learning in life. It offers a place you can hold a deliberate, thoughtful conversation with yourself." – Robin Sharma

---

IF YOU DON'T LIKE
{ SOMETHING, }
CHANGE IT.
IF YOU CAN'T CHANGE IT,
CHANGE YOUR ATTITUDE
-MAYA ANGELOU

SECTION

1

THE FOUNDATION PLAN

"The best foundation anyone can build in life is a mindset that is unwavering when the storm rages."

–Oscar Bimpong

SECTION INTRODUCTION

When building a home, it is critical for the foundation of the house to be steady and stable. The entire home sits on top of the foundation. If it is unable to hold up, the house will eventually crumble.

The same can be said about life. If the foundation we build on is not steady and stable, it is likely that things will start to crumble. In this section we will cover the 5 FOUNDATION KEYS which are The Why, A Different You, The Formula to Success, Creating Your Own Luck, and Trusting the Process.

As you make your transition to and through college, these keys will help you establish the foundation needed to be successful. These keys have been and continue to be essential in helping me reach new levels. Various life experiences have inspired each one of these foundation keys. Within each key, you will find value! These 5 Foundation Keys will help you develop purpose, increase self-awareness, set goals, and guide you towards your next level!

"Adversity causes some people to break and causes others to break records" —Inky Johnson

---

CHAPTER ONE

THE WHY

"Once you act on your passion, you will walk into your purpose" —Blake Simon

WHY COLLEGE?

We are in the times where our economy is stimulated by technology and innovation. As a result, higher education has become more significant than ever. ***Higher education*** is education beyond high school, particularly at a college or university. Students who choose to pursue a higher education usually look to become knowledgeable in a specific field, receive training, and earn a degree or certificate to gain employment in a specific area after graduating.

Students who receive a higher education typically reap financial and personal benefits throughout their lifetime. I am not indicating that you must go to college to be successful. However, an increasing number of jobs require higher education, which can be contributed to factors such as a more globalized economy and the changing labor market.

College provides opportunities that will stimulate personal and professional growth. This stimulation could result in the exploration of new ideas, a better understanding of the world, and much more! Simply put, higher education provides more opportunity. Even the most successful entrepreneurs, entertainers, and athletes have pursued and acquired a higher education to enhance their skill set and opportunities. The objective is to be efficient in the pursuit, and that is what this tool is designed to help you accomplish.

DEVELOPING YOUR WHY

Deciding to go to college is just the first step. Then the journey begins. Preparation for college is a process that should start well before a student steps foot on campus. Some families are intentional about areas such as saving money for college and may begin planning for that process well before their child is even born, while some families may not be able to save for college. Regardless of your individual circumstance, your goal must be to maximize any available resource that will help you become successful throughout your journey. Especially if the odds aren't in your favor! You do not have time to waste!

To truly succeed at anything in life, you must operate with purpose. When you move with purpose, you know exactly

"WHY" you make the moves you make. If you move without purpose, it becomes challenging to make progress in life.

College is a huge step. Too often I've witnessed the students who transition into college without true purpose struggle to remain focused. That lack of focus often translates into failing grades, which typically results in academic probations and suspensions. If you go to college without purpose, you will struggle. If you don't develop purpose quickly, your chances of experiencing success is limited.

Keep this in mind. It is very easy to become susceptible to distractions when you don't have the WHY. Without purpose, any distraction will seem more enticing despite knowing your focus should be elsewhere. Also, somewhere along your journey, you will be faced with adversity. That is life. The key is how you respond to adversity when it presents itself. When you have a purpose attached to your journey, it makes it easier to handle adversity and to deal with distractions.

My objective for you as a student is to help you develop purpose at as early as possible. I started figuring out my WHY at age 28. It was at that point I began to evaluate my *3 Points of Purpose*.

1. The people who have sacrificed for me.

So many people have sacrificed for me to get where I am today. I was born in 1987 when the crack cocaine epidemic was making a hard impact on the African American communities. My biological parents were involved with drugs, and as a result, I was not raised by them. Most children born in those circumstances were raised by aunts, older siblings, and in most cases grandparents. Others who weren't raised by family members were in the foster care system. In my case, it was a little different. From the time I was an infant, I was raised by a woman who had no blood relation to me. She never legally adopted me or became my legal guardian, but she loved me to death.

She was in her early forties at the time and was from what my generation referred to as the "old school." Her foundation was discipline and education. She held to those values while raising me. I knew that there were consequences for my actions. I knew that there were consequences to misbehaving in school. I also knew that I would be rewarded when I performed well.

Despite the circumstances, her willingness to sacrifice for me was undeniable. Even in bad health, she took care of me. When she moved, I moved with her. That was my best friend. On her birthday in July of 1998, she passed away due to health complications. I was eleven years of age.

When I think about the effort she gave in addition to others that have sacrificed for me such as my sister who took care of me once my Mama passed away, I have no choice but to give maximum effort every day as I transition through life. I *grind* to create a legacy that those who have sacrificed for me will be proud of. Grind is exuding great work ethic. As you make your transition, I encourage you to always think about the people who have sacrificed for you throughout your journey.

2. The people who depend on me

As a first-generation college graduate, I understand the significance of setting a positive example and how influential that has been to people who follow in my footsteps. I have siblings, nieces, nephews, and others who look up to me and follow the example I set.

Attending and completing college has had a direct impact on some of my younger siblings and other family members who now KNOW that it is a reality. Many of my siblings were raised in separate households but are influenced by the decisions I make. As I consider the enormous responsibility, I must set positive examples, I allow it to be a motivating factor as I continue my pursuit of greatness. I grind to create a legacy for those who depend on me.

When adversity happens or when you lack motivation, I

encourage you to consider the people who look up to you and depend on you. Someone may be watching you, and you may not know it. Your success could change the landscape of your family and even impact the world.

3. Personal Impact

Once I identified my purpose in this world, everything changed. Life is different when you wake up with purpose. I am on a mission to impact youth based on my personal and professional life experiences. How I impact youth may change throughout my life, but I will always be hugely motivated by the power of my gift to affect lives. I understand that my gift gives me the ability to change the world and I am driven by that every day.

I urge you to figure your purpose in this world and allow it to motivate you daily. The more you tap into your purpose and begin to live it, the less time you will have for distractions.

"Turn your wounds into wisdom."
—Oprah Winfrey

EXERCISE 1

WHAT IS YOUR WHY?

As we have discussed, possessing the ability to identify your WHY is one of the most critical steps in establishing the foundation you need to make any transition in life, so before we continue... what's your WHY? To help you get started, we will explore your "3 Point of Purpose". Answer the following questions.

List 3 reasons why pursuing higher education is important to you?

1. _____

2. _____

3. _____

List 3 people who love you.

1. _____

2. _____

3. _____

List 3 people you love.

1._____

2._____

3._____

What IMPACT do you want to have on the world?

_____

_____

_____

If you weren't sure before, you have now identified several reasons "why" you must remain extremely focused as you make any Transition in life. These people you listed are depending on you. Your future is depending on you. YOU are depending on you!

Congratulations, you are now moving with a purpose!

CHAPTER TWO

A DIFFERENT YOU

"Change will not come if we wait for some other person or some other time. We are the ones we've been waiting for. We are the change that we seek."

—*President Barack Obama*

Making any transition requires A DIFFERENT YOU! The effort that it took for you to get through junior high, high school, or any other level will not be enough to get it done on the next level. YOU must be willing to give more and go all in for your future if you want to achieve long term success.

YOU must be willing to do what you don't want to do **NOW**, to do what you want to in the **FUTURE**. That may mean cutting certain people out. That may mean cutting certain things out. It WILL mean holding yourself accountable to do the things you say you want to do.

You are responsible for making it to every class and excelling in each class. It is you who must eliminate the distractions that are preventing you from transitioning to your next level. It is on you to land the job you want to land.

It is all on YOU! Hold yourself accountable!

Once again, it's not going to be easy, but you have what it takes to make it happen! If you want to be successful on any level, now is the time to activate A DIFFERENT YOU!

"If my mind can conceive it, and my heart can believe it, then I can achieve it." – Muhammad Ali

---

Your thoughts will attract things to you, but just envisioning what you want is not enough. You must put in the WORK! You must become consumed with your goals like you do with anything else you are really into. For some, it may be sports, video games, television, or social media. The things we are interested in will quickly take up hours out of our day, and that's fine.

The objective is to line up your **priorities** and dedicate time to the things that will contribute to your overall success. A priority is something that has a high level of importance and must be dealt with before other things. It shouldn't be hard to move YOUR future to the top of YOUR priority list.

You must believe in yourself if you want to be successful in life. If you don't believe in yourself, now is the time to remove all self-doubt and negative thinking. Don't question your desires. Your life can be the way you envision it to be! Continue to visualize what you want out of life.

You must envision yourself where you want to be and start living the part now. Some people may refer to that as "Faking it until you make it," but if you're going to be successful, you must carry yourself like you are already where you want to be. If you're going to be a millionaire, you must have a million-dollar mindset. If you're going to be an Engineer, you are an Engineer. In your mind, you must be there already. You're not faking it; you're embodying it. It's the Law of Attraction! Attract SUCCESS! Become consumed with it and work towards achieving it every day.

As I maneuver through transitions in my life, something that I find to be effective is creating positive **_affirmations_**.

An affirmation is a statement asserting the existence or truth of something. I encourage you to create positive affirmations and declare that whatever you want out of life is already a reality. So, I ask you, what do you want for yourself?

Using the next exercise, I want you to create 15 positive affirmations. Don't cheat yourself!

EXERCISE 2

POSITIVE AFFIRMATIONS

To help you get started, check out 15 positive affirmations I created for myself.

1. I wake up every day with a strong heart and a clear mind.

2. My faith in myself is unwavering.

3. Wealth flows into my life.

4. I change lives.

5. I make decisions that positively impact my future.

6. I surround myself with positive people.

7. I live a healthy lifestyle.

8. My business ventures flourish.

9. I travel the world.

10. I have an amazing family.

11. My future is what I envision it to be.

12. I am debt free.

13. I help develop the next generation of leaders.

14. I collaborate with Mrs. Michelle Obama to prepare students for college.

15. I wake up blessed every day.

Use the space provided to create a list of positive affirmations that will change your life!

Affirmation #1

_____

_____

Affirmation #2

_____

_____

Affirmation #3

_____

_____

Affirmation #4

_____

_____

Affirmation #5

_____

_____

Affirmation #6

_____

_____

Affirmation #7

_____

_____

Affirmation #8

_____

_____

Affirmation #9

_____

_____

Affirmation #10

_____

_____

Affirmation #11

_____

_____

Affirmation #12

_____

_____

Affirmation #13

_____

_____

Affirmation #14

_____

_____

Affirmation #15

_____

_____

CHAPTER THREE

THE FORMULA TO SUCCESS

"Setting goals is the first step in turning the invisible into the visible." –Tony Robbins

Growing up, I always equated success to tangible things such as clothes, shoes, cars, and money. I always thought that if you had those things, you were successful. As I grew older, I realize that I was wrong.

Success is not about tangible items, but more about achievement. To achieve, you must set **goals**. A goal is an idea of your future or the desired result that you envision, plan, and commit to achieving.

So the formula to success is simple.

CREATING GOALS

The first step in my formula to success is Goal Setting. Creating goals will take you from mediocre to good and from good to great. As a student, the goals you create should align with your life vision.

For example, if you are going to be a Nurse, your goals should align with that vision. Ask yourself these questions. Do I know what courses are required to acquire this degree? Are there any summer programs for future Nurses? Have I researched internships? Do I have a mentor that is a Nurse? What salary do I desire? What organizations are great to work with or for?

Create short-term and long-term goals. Establish goals for today, next week, next year and five years from now!

ACCOMPLISHING THE GOALS

Goals are created to accomplish. As you begin to accomplish goals, you will introduce success into your life. Soon you will develop a system built on habits that generate success. The more goals you accomplish, the more goals you create. The more SUCCESS you achieve! It seems easy, right? You may be wondering why more people aren't successful if it's that easy. Well, that answer is simple as well. It is not easy.

It's going to take faith, consistency, and hard work. Most people aren't willing to trust the process. But remember, you have what it takes to make it happen. You must be willing to put in the work and *grind*. Everything else will fall into place!

EXERCISE 3
TEN M.A.P. GOALS

To get you started on your pathway to success, I want you to establish the top TEN goals you will accomplish as you make your transition to and/or through college. For accountability purposes, indicate how you will accomplish each goal and establish a deadline for each goal. See the example below for guidance.

Goal: Find a Mentor in my field of study
How: Build effective relationships with professors and connect with professionals at career fairs.
Deadline: By the end of freshman year

This exercise is merely a starter to get you in the habit of setting and accomplishing goals, but you must remain consistent and persistent if you want to be successful. Use the journal space provided throughout the book to write more goals as you make your Transition and build successful habits.

1. Goal

_____

_____

How will you accomplish this goal?

_____

_____

Deadline: _____

2. Goal

_____

_____

How will you accomplish this goal?

_____

_____

Deadline: _____

3. Goal

_____

_____

How will you accomplish this goal?

_____

_____

Deadline: _____

4. Goal

_____

_____

How will you accomplish this goal?

_____

_____

Deadline: _____

5. Goal

_____

_____

How will you accomplish this goal?

_____

_____

Deadline: _____

6. Goal

_____

_____

How will you accomplish this goal?

_____

_____

Deadline: _____

7. Goal

_____

_____

How will you accomplish this goal?

_____

_____

Deadline: _____

8. Goal

_____

_____

How will you accomplish this goal?

_____

_____

Deadline: _____

9. Goal

_____

_____

How will you accomplish this goal?

_____

_____

Deadline: _____

10. Goal

_____

_____

How will you accomplish this goal?

_____

_____

Deadline: _____

CHAPTER FOUR

CREATE YOUR OWN LUCK

"If a window of opportunity appears, don't pull down the shade." —Thomas Peters

During my second semester of college, my government professor made a statement before a test that I would never forget. He said, "I would say good luck, but luck is when PREPARATION meets OPPORTUNITY, and I know you all are prepared". Once he distributed the test, it became clear to me what he meant. The students who were not prepared did not do as well on the test. The students who were prepared excelled on the test, and it wasn't because of LUCK. It was because of PREPARATION!

PREPARATION

The process of becoming READY for SOMETHING is referred to as *preparation*. Successful people prepare themselves to be in that position. Athletes, Musicians, Teachers, Students, and anyone else who reaches any level of success prepares for it.

In some cases, the preparation phase may not be the most

enjoyable experience. In fact, it requires extreme sacrifice. It may mean doing what others won't do. It may be discouraging, and it will be challenging, but you must push through and tap into the "Why". The objective is to prepare and always stay ready for the opportunities that will come your way.

OPPORTUNITY

There is a WINDOW of time when SOMETHING can be done to improve your circumstances. That is an *opportunity*. When that window presents itself, the work you put in during the preparation phase will be exposed. You will either be ready for the moment or that window will close without you.

Opportunity is something you must not take for granted. It may come and then elude you for years or even a lifetime. If you pay close attention in life, you will notice that the "veteran" always tells the "rookie" to take advantage of the moment because you never know if it will come again. That is true and real. Always stay prepared and be ready to maximize every opportunity!

CREATE YOUR OWN LUCK!

CHAPTER FIVE

TRUST THE PROCESS

"Success is not for the weak and uncommitted...
Sometimes it's gonna hurt!" –Eric Thomas

The foundation is almost complete, but there is one final key. You must TRUST THE PROCESS. Over a year had passed since high school graduation, and I had not identified my passionate or purpose in life. I had not enrolled at a college or university. I didn't have a career path or a consistent job. I tried to figure things out, but my lack of focus and limited guidance in high school had me in a lost place. I didn't see the light at the end of the tunnel.

A friend and former high school teammate of mine who attended a local university was still around so we would hang out from time to time. One day, he indicated that he was thinking about transferring to Prairie View A&M University (PVAMU). He then suggested that I make a move as well. This conversation about college was different and sparked my interest. I knew I had to make something happen, so I started the process of admitting into PVAMU.

I had no idea what I wanted to major in or what career

path to explore. At that point, I just needed to do something that I thought was meaningful. In January 2007, I enrolled at Prairie View A&M University. That decision changed my life forever. The College experience was like no other. I was able to evolve as a young man and as a student. Since then, I've completed my undergraduate studies receiving a Bachelor of Science in Criminal Justice and a Master of Arts in Counseling. I've also identified passion and purpose while establishing a career in education. I accomplished these goals while overcoming much adversity, so I know that anything you put your mind and grind to is possible.

Trusting the process embodies everything that we have discussed thus far such as knowing your why, getting better every day, goal setting, and preparation. Also, there are three more keys that help you successfully make the transition.

1. HAVE FAITH

You must have *faith* in yourself. To have faith is to have complete trust or confidence in someone or something. Before you expect anyone else to have faith in your dreams, you must believe it. Have faith that whatever it is you want to do in life is possible because it is. Be logical of course but dream big and believe! If you don't believe in yourself, now is the time to remove all self-doubt and negative thinking. Don't question your abilities and aspirations. Have FAITH!

2. TAKE ACTION

Your life can be the way you envision it to be, but you must *take action*. Taking action is about putting in the work to accomplish your goals. Having faith is one thing, but you must grind to see results. In high school, I had this false sense of security where I thought everything would work itself out. My mistake was I needed to "work" things out. I needed to put in more work for the things I wanted. Have faith in your abilities and aspiration, and then take ACTION!

3. REMAIN CONSISTENT

Last but not least, you must remain consistent! *Consistency* is your action over a period of time. You have the power to determine what that action will be. Will you choose to be consistently lazy or consistently successful? Consistency separates successful students and visionaries from the rest. Even with faith and action, a lack of consistency will derail your success. It requires a tremendous amount of discipline to remain consistent, but you must remember the reasons "why" you do it. Have FAITH, take ACTION, and remain CONSISTENT! I truly believe that each person has something special within them. We all have a gift! The key is unlocking your gift and mastering it. You master it by putting in the work and trusting the process. If you do, you will reap the benefits. You have what it takes to make the transition and pass any test life throws your way!

ACTIVATE YOUR

D.A.W.G. MENTALITY

DETERMINATION AGGRESSION WILLINGNESS GRIT

I CAN'T RELATE TO LAZY PEOPLE.

WE DONT

SPEAK THE

SAME LANGUAGE

{ -KOBE BRYANT }

JOURNAL NOTES

_____

_____

_____

_____

_____

_____

_____

_____

_____

_____

_____

_____

_____

_____

SECTION

2

THE ACADEMIC PLAN

"Education is the passport to the future, for tomorrow belongs to those who prepare for it today" –Malcolm X

SECTION INTRODUCTION

Now that you have laid the Foundation of your Master Action Plan (MAP), we will focus on the Academic Plan. Some students begin their pursuit of higher education with intention and purpose. They know what major they will select and the career field they will enter. Others start their quest for higher education with less clarity and are undecided regarding their field of study. Regardless of the circumstance, every student can finish college at the highest level. Once again, the key is preparation. As you make your transition, consider and utilize the academic success keys discussed throughout this section.

CHAPTER SIX

COLLEGE & BEYOND

"If you have no confidence in self, you are twice defeated in the race of life." —Marcus Garvey

SELECTING MAJOR & CAREER OUTLOOK

In section one, I encouraged you to explore your purpose which is critical to keep in mind as you evaluate career interest, selecting a major, and your desired lifestyle.

LIFESTYLE & INTEREST

Transitioning to and through college is a vital part of life, but you must always think about the long game. As you explore career options and selecting a major, it is essential to learn about yourself. Explore your values, interest, and skills. Also, keep in mind the questions you answered in section one *Know Your Why*. Mainly, what impact do you want to have on the world?

The idea is to align your interest with purpose. When thinking about your future, ask yourself the following questions. Do I want a family? Where do I want to live? How much do I want my annual salary to be? As you think about each component of your long-term plan, you will notice that each one impacts the other. After evaluating each area, compare those to the characteristics of majors and careers.

CAREER

Ultimately, your **career** choice could be the most critical decision you encounter because this may be where and how you'll spend most of your time. A career is the occupation assume for a significant period of your life and with opportunities for progress.

For some people, career paths change throughout life. For others, they can explore their passion and identify their purpose at an earlier stage in life. If you haven't determined your career path, use self-assessment tools, gather information about your personality traits and move forward with narrowing down on a list of suitable occupations. Also, speak with a career counselor and/or other career development professionals who can help you navigate this process.

As you transition to and through college, seek out opportunities that will increase your levels of success in your desired career field. For example, Build Effective Relationships & Network which is something we will discuss in this section. Also, take advantage of opportunities to gain experience in your desired field. Seek out the relative job, internship, and volunteer opportunities.

MAJOR

The reality is most students are faced with deciding on a *major* before they have figured out their purpose in life. Your major is the subject or field of study you choose to represent your principal interest and upon which a large share of your efforts are concentrated.

I believe that you should choose a major that interests you and that will lead to a purposeful career. Some majors include agriculture, nursing, engineering, or education. Each specific major is outlined through what is called a ***degree plan***. Your degree plan is specific to your major and is created in collaboration with your academic advisor. It is the required coursework necessary to graduate. Your degree plan should detail what classes you will take and when. As you transition to and through college, you will work with an Academic Advisor (see *Campus Resources*) to develop and execute your degree plan.

DEGREE TYPES

As you begin your pursuit of higher education, it is critical to familiarize yourself with the types of degrees available based on your level of education completed.

Associate Degree: This 2-year degree is an Associate of Arts (A.A.) or Associate of Science (A.S.). Some students who earn this degree transfer to a 4-year program to earn a bachelor's degree. Others complete associate degrees to prepare to go straight to work. Community colleges, career colleges, and some four-year colleges offer these degrees. Typically, ***60 hours*** required.

Bachelor's (or Baccalaureate) Degree: This degree requires completing a 4- or 5-year college program. Most students earn a Bachelor of Arts (B.A.) or Bachelor of Science degree (B.S.). Typically, ***120 hours*** required.

Graduate Degree: Graduate degrees are advanced degrees pursued after earning a bachelor's degree. Examples are a Master of Arts (M.A.) or Master of Science (M.S.) degree. Students generally can earn a master's degree after two years of study. Typically, ***36-54 hours*** required.

Doctoral Degree: A doctorate is the highest level of academic degree. A doctoral degree (for example, a Ph.D.) may require 4 or more years of study. You may also be familiar with a medical doctor, who holds a Medical Doctorate (M.D.) typically ***90-120 hours*** required.

** There are also other types of degrees and certifications such as a Professional Degree and Liberal Arts degrees.

COURSE TYPE

Basic Core courses are typically required regardless of major. These courses may include English, Math, History, or Government.

Major Core courses are directly related to the major. For example, a student majoring in Business Management may be required to take major courses such as Quantitative Business Analysis or Principles of Finance.

Elective courses aren't directly related to your major but are required. When choosing an elective course, you have freer will to choose an alternative course of interest. For example, a Nursing student who is interested in taking a Business course would have the opportunity to take the course as an elective.

COURSE SELECTION

Course selection in college should be approached strategically and with intention. Always remember the primary objective which is to complete the course work required to obtain the degree. The best method of efficiency to stay on course for graduation is to establish a degree plan and execute.

If you haven't decided on a major, stick to the basic core

classes like English, Government I & II, History I & II, and General Electives until you decide on a major. This strategy can prevent you from wasting money and time taking courses you won't need. If you have decided on a major, it would be best to get those basic core classes out the way while mixing in entry-level major core classes.

Each course is typically worth three credit hours except for some classes such as labs which may be worth one credit hour. Twelve credit hours are considered a full-time course load. If you are aiming to take a full load, consider taking 4 (12 credit hours) to 6 (18 credit hours) each semester. I would suggest that you take no more than 15 credits hours during your first semester. Classes that are 3 days a week are typically fifty minutes to an hour. Courses that are two days a week or 1 day a week usually have longer meeting times. Some colleges and universities offer online classes and programs. You should approach online courses with the same intention.

The overall objective is to maintain balance. You may want to take challenging classes as a freshman, but I would suggest working your way up to the more difficult courses. Be aware of the types of classes you are taking and the workload that is required for each class. Also, spread your easier electives out to alleviate your workload each semester as you progress through your degree plan. In addition, always register early. Be aware of registration dates by checking the registration calendar on your college or university website. Registering early gives you the opportunity to pick classes at the time and days you want which will help to balance out your schedule.

GRADING FORMULA

A *grade point average (GPA)* is a number representing the average value of the accumulated final grades earned in courses each semester and over time. The GPA is calculated by adding up all accumulated final grades and dividing that figure by the number of grades awarded.

Total Points Earned

_____ = **Grade Point Average**

Total Class/Grade Attempts

Grading Percentages

A = 100- 90   4 points per semester hour
B = 89 - 80:   3 points per semester hour
C = 79 - 70:   2 points per semester hour

D = 69 - 60:   1 point per semester hour
F = 59 and below   0 points per semester hour

W (Withdrawn)   0 points per semester hour
I (Incomplete)   0 points per semester hour

Here is an example of how to calculate your GPA.

Course	Grade	Points Earned
Algebra	C	2
History	B	3
English	A	4
Intro to Business	B	3
Biology	D	1

13 Total points earned

——————————————— = **2.6 GPA**

5 Total classes/grade attempts

In this example, the student is taking five classes in total and earned 13 total grade points. The student's overall grade points earned (13) divided by the 5 class/grade attempts means the student has a GPA of 2.6.

This is the method I used throughout my college transition, but there may be other ways to calculate your GPA depending on the point scale and how many credit hours the class is worth. Follow up with your *Academic Advisor* for clarity.

EXERCISE 4

PLAN YOUR NEXT TWO SEMESTERS

As we discussed in section I, preparation is key! Planning your semester is a critical success strategy that you need to develop. Once again, as you transition to and through college, you will work with an *Academic Advisor* to develop and execute your degree plan, but you are responsible for doing the planning first. In preparation for the upcoming semesters, use the following diagram to plan out the courses you will take. Visit your university or college website to find a copy of the suggested degree plan for your major as guidance. See the example below.

Course Title and #	Credit Earned	Course Type	Notes
English I 1000	3	Basic Core	Take ENG II in Spring
Algebra I 1200	3	Basic Core	n/a
Theatre Arts 3000	3	Arts Elective	1 Arts left
Intro to Business 2000	3	Major Core	n/a
History I 1500	3	Basic Core	Take HIST II in spring
SEMESTER CREDITS: 15		HOURS TO GRADUATE: **105 (120 total)**	

PLAN YOUR NEXT TWO SEMESTERS

Course Title and #	Credit Earned	Course Type	Notes
SEMESTER CREDITS EARNED:		HOURS TO GRADUATE:	

Course Title and #	Credit Earned	Course Type	Notes
SEMESTER CREDITS EARNED:		HOURS TO GRADUATE:	

QUICK KEYS

1. Make time for yourself.
2. Protect your reputation.
3. Stay connected with your close family.
4. Stay in contact with your close friends.
5. Eliminate distractions.
6. Stay on campus for at least one year.
7. Find a Mentor in your prospective field.
8. Become efficient using the Microsoft Office (Word, Excel, PowerPoint, & Outlook).
9. Find great study partners who share your major.
10. ALWAYS read your class syllabus as soon as you get it.
11. Keep your Grade Point Average (GPA) up. If your GPA drops, it is difficult to bring up.
12. Avoid paying full price for books. Check online or with students that previously took the course for cheaper prices.
13. Learn how to write in the required format. Most college/universities require students to utilize APA (American Psychological Association) writing style.
14. Don't cheat! Consequences for cheating are severe.
15. Wikipedia is not a credible source for research papers
16. Complete your own degree audit each semester.
17. Strategically plan out your summers to avoid wasting time.
18. Don't wear pajamas to class.
19. Start saving money if you haven't already.

Take College serious from the very first day.
College Days Swiftly Pass!

CHAPTER SEVEN

KEY CAMPUS RESOURCES

"You can't be a resource for others unless you nourish yourself." —Alexandra Stoddard

It is quite possible that while in college you will have more resources at your fingertips than any other time in life. Most of these resources, if not all, are paid for in your tuition and fees.

It is critical to take advantage of the resources you are paying for. In this section, we will cover several key ***campus recourses*** that will help make your Transition easier and help you maximize your college experience in general.

EXERCISE 5
LOCATE THE RESOURCE

As we navigate through each campus resource, you will be required to list the exact building location for each resource on your current or prospective campus.

LIBRARY

The campus library is one of the most important resources available to you on a college campus. Reading and research is key to a success in college. The library is full of educational resources that can be used to increase your knowledge in various areas in addition to your field of study. Be sure to connect with the campus librarian(s). They are very resourceful and knowledgeable.

Most campus libraries have an open computer lab for students who don't own a personal laptop and to print assignments, projects, and more. The library is a great place to meet for study sessions. You may also check with the library to see if your course book is available to check out. Lastly, utilize your college/university library to access online databases such as EBSCOhost & JSTOR for research.

What building is the Library located in on your campus?

_____

ACADEMIC ADVISING CENTER

Academic advising is critical to your Transition through college. Your academic advisor will help guide you with your course selection and assist you with your degree plan. Many colleges and universities have different advising models.

Your advisor may be a faculty member or a professional advisor. Sometimes advisors are assigned through your major or department. Find out who is your academic advisor based on your school's advising model. You should already have your courses picked out before you meet with your advisor. Your advisor should be verifying and making suggestions if necessary. Do not depend on them to do it for you. Your advisor is there to GUIDE you. Also, always have your questions ready when meeting with an advisor.

Where is the Academic Advising Center or your Academic Advisor located on your campus?

_____

BUSINESS (FINANCIAL) SERVICES

The Business office, which is also known as Treasury Services or Financial Services on some campuses, is there to assist students with their tuition & fee billing, issue student refunds, billing statements, 1098-T forms and receive and manage all incoming funds for the college/university.

What building is Business Services located in on your campus?

FINANCIAL AID & SCHOLARSHIPS

One of the most important departments to become familiar with is The Office of Financial Aid & Scholarships. I will expound on the financial aid process in section III, but The Office of Scholarships and Financial Aid provides students with financial assistance through grants, loans, scholarships, and federal work-study employment. It should always be a priority to stay connected with a financial aid representative.

What building is the Financial Aid Office located in on your campus?

CAREER SERVICES CENTER

Planning a visit to the campus career center should be at the top of your campus to-do list. The career center can to prepare you for the Transition from college to career through programs and services. This resource also allows you to connect with employers for jobs, internships, co-ops, and career opportunities.

Start utilizing this resource as a freshman. Don't wait until your senior year in college to visit the career services center. The career services center staff should know you by name.

You should be the first person that comes to mind when an opportunity comes up that fits you.

What building is the Career Services located in on your campus?

_____

TUTORING CENTER

The tutoring center is a resource that many students fail to take advantage of. If you are having trouble in a specific subject area, USE THIS SERVICE! Most centers will offer free face-to-face tutoring for their students. The tutoring center usually has faculty tutors, peer tutors and lab aides that are available to help with English, Math, Biology, Physics, Chemistry, Accounting, Spanish, ESOL, and much more. This center can help you stay on track with your coursework, understand assignments, and improve your study skills. Be sure to utilize this resource if you need it!

What building is the Tutoring Center located in on your campus?

_____

WRITING CENTER

As you Transition from high school to college, the writing requirements may change (e. g. APA). Writing centers are a place for you to get help with any aspect of writing, from specific assignments to general writing skills. Writing centers are usually staffed with trained undergraduate and faculty tutors who provide individual conferences to students working on any writing assignment. This center is an excellent resource for when you need to finish a paper. Visit the center with your assignment requirements, ideas, notes, and a draft if you have one.

What building is the Writing Center located in on your campus?

COUNSELING CENTER

The counselling center is staffed with licensed, skilled professionals who are there to assist students who are dealing with academic skills concerns, situational crises, adjustment problems, and emotional difficulties. Information shared with the staff is treated confidentially and in accordance with State Law. Most campus counseling services provide short-term individual, couples, and group counseling, as well as crisis intervention, outreach, consultation, and referral services. Some counseling centers offer extremely informative educational workshops and classroom presentations to interested groups who request them.

What building is the Counseling Center located in on your campus?

HEALTH CENTER

The campus health center is available to provide professional medical care, health education and health promotion for students. The centers are there to help with illness or any other physical issue you might face while away at school. They are staffed with competent medical personnel to address any need you might have. If they deem it an emergency, they can arrange for further treatment at a hospital affiliated or close by to the campus.

What building is the Health Center located in on your campus?

STUDENT RECREATION CENTER

The campus rec center is a great place to get a workout in and maintain your health. The campus rec center may have programs such as Fitness & Wellness, Intramural Sports, Club Sports, Informal Recreation and much more. Resources may vary depending on your college or university, but you should consider taking advantage of what is available to you.

What building is the Student Recreation Center located in on your campus?

_____

STUDENT LIFE

Personal development will be very critical as you Transition to and through college. Joining a student organization can be a life-changing experience. It helped me increased my leadership skills, speaking ability, self-confidence, time management skills, and more. Becoming a student leader can equip you with various skills that can be utilized after college such as running a business and building a network.

Joining a student organization and getting involved on

campus may come with some perks. Some student leaders in positions such as Student Body President and Vice President sometimes receive free campus housing. Getting involved on campus may also provide opportunities to see different cities, states, and even countries. Students travel through clubs, sports, band, dance teams, and a multitude of other student organizations for various reasons.

*Quick Tip: If you are interested in combining education with travel, seek out study abroad and exchange student programs that may exist on your campus.

What building is Student Life located in on your campus?

_____

COLLEGE/UNIVERSITY WEBSITE

One of the most important resources is the university/college website. Most of your questions can be answered by visiting the site. You can find information about your degree program, registration dates, directories, financial aid, and much more. Please utilize your school's site when you have questions. If you are not able to get someone via phone or email, please check the website and use the search box to see if you can answer your own question(s).

There are more campus resources available for you as you make you Transition to and through college. You must seek out these resources and use them to your advantage!

List your College/University website domain below.

_____

CHAPTER EIGHT

NETWORKING & RELATIONSHIPS

"I've learned that people will forget what you said, people will forget what you did, but people will never forget how you made them feel."
—*Maya Angelou*

Networking and building relationships are two of the most important aspects of life. Students who actively network and building effective relationships experience more success in college and beyond. **Networking** is the action or process of interacting with others to exchange information and develop a professional or social relationship. A **relationship** is a way in which two or more people or things are connected. Networking is the first step to building an EFFECTIVE relationship.

INTENTIONAL NETWORKING

As you are exposed to opportunities to meet new people, you are exposed to opportunities to build a new relationship. Always look to position yourself around people with experience or people with similar goals. Your career and life goals should influence and inspire your networking efforts while in college. For example, if you are pursuing a career in Education, it is important to focus on building relationships with individuals and entities in the Education community.

Networking and building effective relationships will often open doors for opportunities to gain experience in your desired career field. A networking opportunity could translate into an internship, co-op, or volunteer opportunity.

An **internship** is an opportunity for a student to gain a professional learning experience related to their field of study or career interest. Internships can be a paid or unpaid opportunity.

Cooperative education (Co-op) combines practical work experience with classroom-based education and is typically a paid opportunity lasting anywhere from 2 to 12 months.

A **volunteer** serves. Volunteering can be very beneficial as it pertains to gaining experience, knowledge, and building connections. On the other hand, volunteering requires less of a commitment, and you are not likely to advance to more difficult learning situations. Selecting a quality volunteer experience is recommended.

If you are in a field that will require experience, this is especially important for you. Experience not only builds your brand, skills, and reputation, but it also enhances your *résumé*. Your résumé is a document indicating your experience, skills, and accomplishments. You will need a résumé for a variety of reasons, but most often they are used to secure employment opportunities.

Networking also creates an opportunity to obtain a *mentor* in your field. A mentor is a person who provides a less experienced person with guidance and advice over a period of time, especially pertaining to career and education.

BUILDING RELATIONSHIPS WITH PROFESSORS

College professors are not like your high school teachers. It is important to understand this because it will help you build a better relationship with your professors. It's a little different in college. Professors may have the responsibility of advising students, running a laboratory or department, and performing service. In addition, some professors are conducting research, publishing papers, writing grant proposals, and furthering their education.

In other words, teaching may not be the only concern for SOME college professors. This does not mean that they aren't excellent teachers, but it does mean you need to know how to interact with your professors to get the most out of the class and build an effective relationship.

Here are a few pointers:

- **Do your part in class.** Come to every class, sit towards the front of the class, and participate in class. You want your professor to know your face for great reasons. Also, take effective *notes*. Utilize a note-taking style such as Cornell, Paragraphing, Listing, or Outlining.

- **Show interest in lectures** and ask about their research (if any). If you are genuinely interested in that subject, ask if you could assist in the lab. This will help increase your knowledge and skills in that area. Professors in fields like science, agriculture, and engineering may even be able to pay you as a student worker.

- **Take advantage of office hours**. Few students take advantage of office hours... early in the semester. Utilize office hours if you are not clear on the content being discussed in the course and as an opportunity for one-on-one mentoring from an expert.

Building a great relationship with your professors can go a long way. For example, you may need a reference or recommendation in the future, and your professor is more likely to consider recommending or referring you if you exude great work ethic and exceptional character.

Throughout my time in college, I established several effective relationships with several professors and other professionals on campus. As a result of maintaining those relationships through college and beyond, I have been able to rely on those contacts as recommendations or references for various opportunities.

PROFESSIONAL REFERENCES

At all times, it would be in your best interest to have at least *3 professional references*. A professional reference is a recommendation from a person who can vouch for your qualifications for a job, scholarship, or organization membership. Professional references could include professors, counselors, administrators, coaches, past supervisors, and any other professionals who would vouch for your character and ability. For anyone to vouch for you, there must be a relationship established. You should not expect anyone to put their name on the line for you if you have not showcased the ability to perform at a certain level.

For example, during my first semester in college, I had an 8 A.M. class across campus. I didn't see anything unique about the time of the class because I had always been a morning person, but as I progressed through college, I realized most students made a conscious effort to stay away from early morning classes. Nonetheless, that was the first class I stepped foot into as a college student, so my mindset was to set the tone! I started on a high note and maintained that effort throughout the first few weeks, but I realized most of my classmates began to fall off. Some started to come late; some simply stopped coming.

Eventually, the professor pulled a classmate and me aside to recognize the effort we were giving in the class. She pointed out that we sat on the front row, participated, and were consistently on time. She followed up with saying that we would earn an "A" in the course if they continued to give the same effort. We did, and we both earned an "A" in the class.

As I transitioned through college, I maintained a productive relationship with her... mainly through office visits. She eventually became the assistant dean of the department. Ultimately, as I completed job applications and pursued employment post-college, that professor did not hesitate to allow me to list her as a professional reference or to write recommendation letters. I am sure my effort in her class put me in a position to have her as a professional reference.

In preparation for future opportunities that may require references or recommendations, always have three professional references. If you do not have three references, I challenge you to get three which will start with networking and building effective relationships. Each time you intend to utilize someone as a professional reference, reach out to the individual to assure that you are still able to list them. Send a courtesy email or place a courtesy phone call. Important reference information to have:

- Name (First and Last)
- Business Email
- Business Phone Number

INTENTIONAL FRIENDSHIPS

It's easy to call anyone your friend, primarily as a first-year student in college. That is not always a great idea. Know what you are looking for in a friend and then find people who fit those qualities. College is a unique time when you are surrounded by hundreds and even thousands of like-minded peers that are your age and on the track for success. You have plenty of positivity to choose from, so stay away from the negative.

Don't focus solely on what you can get from people. Giving value helps build effective relationships. It helps to be there for someone you're close to and can offer a solution. Work on building a solid foundation with the people you do let in your circle. I was intentional about the people I let in my circle, but some of the most fulfilling friendships I have today are with people I met in college.

I want you to understand that there is a difference between having friends and having a network. Of course, my friends are in my network, but so are people I met throughout my time college that aren't my close friends. I refer to them as my "College Network". We work together at times and benefit each other however we can because of the relationship we established while in college.

There is no substitute for networking in college. In my opinion, no skill will be more beneficial to you throughout your college transition. Stay connected to the people you network with and just like everything else, network with a purpose. Be intentional!

EXERCISE 6

10 PEOPLE TO KNOW ON CAMPUS

1. WHO IS THE COLLEGE/UNIVERSITY PRESIDENT?

_____

2. WHO IS THE DEAN OF YOUR COLLEGE (DEPARTMENT)?

_____

3. WHO IS THE ADMINISTRATIVE ASSISTANT TO THE DEAN?

_____

4. WHO IS YOUR ACADEMIC ADVISOR?

_____

5. WHO IS THE DIRECTOR OF FINANCIAL AID?

_____

6. WHO IS YOUR FINANCIAL AID COUNSELOR?

_____

7. WHO IS THE DIRECTOR OF CAREER SERVICES?

_____

8. WHO IS THE HEAD LIBRARIAN?

_____

9. LIST ONE LICENSED PROFESSIONAL COUNSELOR ON CAMPUS.

_____

10. WHO IS THE STUDENT BODY PRESIDENT?

_____

CHAPTER NINE

TIME MANAGEMENT

"Absorb what is useful, reject what is useless, add what is essentially your own." – Bruce Lee

A critical ingredient to success in college and beyond is time management. Everyone has different strategies regarding how they manage time. In fact, some people don't have a strategy at all. Some people are organized and are always on time. There are others who are the exact opposite. I've found that in the past, things I would say I didn't have time for just weren't a priority.

Based on my experiences, I believe the key to time management is organization and prioritizing. As a student, I always keep the main goals in mind and know what is most important. Life comes with responsibilities at all stages. When I was 16 years of age, I started working part-time. I worked on weekends and weekdays after football or baseball practice. That was my first experience with balancing school, work, and personal interest. As I transitioned into college, I became for strategic and efficient with time management.

In college, most students are faced with balancing responsibilities on a different level or in some cases for the first time. As you make your transition, it is essential to know you can accomplish the goals you have set forth. Avoid becoming overwhelmed by having a clear understanding of your daily, weekly, monthly, and semester goals. A less stressful environment is more conducive to success. Let's explore some ways to become more efficient at managing time.

UTILIZE A CALENDAR

A huge key to effective time management is a calendar. Most successful people have a system. It is essential to know what works best for you. For example, some people like to write things down so it would be easier to have a calendar journal or to utilize a resource such as this book. Others prefer to use electronic devices such as smartphones, tablets, and laptops for notes and calendar applications.

I use both methods to stay organized, but my calendar app on my phone has been the most useful resource in recent years. Once you have identified your strength regarding organizing tasks, it is time to evaluate your priorities.

SEMESTER BY SEMESTER

It is a semester by semester grind! As a student making the transition to and through college, use your **syllabus** for each class as the basis for laying out your academic priorities and staying ahead of deadlines. The syllabus is an academic document that details information about each course and defines the expectations and responsibilities of the course.

Also, always be aware to the college or university Academic Calendar which displays dates specific to the school including financial aid, registration, add/drop, midterm/final exam, holiday, and other important dates throughout the semester. Once you gather important dates from your syllabus and academic calendar, also consider any important personal events such as a work schedule, doctors' appointments, birthdays, and more.

DON'T PROCRASTINATE

During my time in college, a major obstacle I had to overcome was **procrastination**. Procrastination is when you have a habit of being slow or late about completing a task that in some cases may need your immediate attention.

Students procrastinate for different reasons. I procrastinated because I knew I could get it done which caused me to delay completing the task! Some of the other reason's students procrastinate include a fear of failure and a lack of motivation.

I challenge you to remind yourself of the "Why" when you notice yourself procrastinating. Also, think about the consequences of procrastination. Essentially, the objective is to stick with your calendar. If you struggle from procrastination, look to become more strategic with planning your daily task. Break your big task down into smaller task by creating daily to-do checklist. Your goal should be to "schedule the day" and not let the day schedule you.

"I DON'T
BELIEVE
IN FAILURE, IT
{ IS NOT FAILURE }
IF YOU ENJOYED
THE PROCESS."
-OPRAH WINFREY

JOURNAL NOTES

_____

_____

_____

_____

_____

_____

_____

_____

_____

_____

_____

_____

_____

_____

_____

_____

_____

_____

_____

_____

_____

_____

_____

_____

_____

_____

_____

SECTION

3

THE FINANCIAL PLAN

"If you want to thrive in today's economy, you must challenge the status quo and get the financial education necessary to succeed." -Robert Kiyosaki

SECTION INTRODUCTION

The final piece to your college M.A.P. is the Financial Plan. Having the ability to create and execute a financial plan will be critical as you make your transition to college, through college, and beyond. Higher education can be costly, and the reality is most students and families lack financial resources to pay for it.

I have found that in addition to limited resources, most students and families lack financial literacy and strategy. As we conclude and navigate through the last section of this book, we will cover two critical financial areas. Financial aid and Budgeting are considerable components to overall financial success in college. Let's begin with Understanding Financial Aid.

CHAPTER TEN

UNDERSTANDING FINANCIAL AID

"Higher education cannot be a luxury reserved just for a privileged few. It is an economic necessity for every family. And every family should be able to afford it." —President Barack Obama

Choosing the best college to attend and creating an academic plan is half of the battle. As you make the transition to and through college, it is just as critical to develop and execute a financial plan.

Year after year, students and families throughout the nation struggle to understand the financial aid process. Resources and literacy are among the top reasons contributing to this struggle. Student loans have left millions of U. S. students in thousands of dollars in student loans debt. As a former student who utilized financial aid and as higher education professional that specialized in financial aid, I understand the rigors this process may cause without adequate financial literacy and strategy.

This portion of the section is designed to give you a better understanding and guide you through those rigors. In the upcoming pages, you will find critical keys that will help you transition through college with an understanding of the financial aid process. What is *financial aid*? Financial Aid is any scholarship, grant, loan, or paid employment offered to help a student pay for college-related expenses.

How to receive Financial Aid?

Financial aid can be received based on **merit** (talents such as academic & athletic abilities) or **need** (family income, assets, and other household information). To determine your NEED, colleges use the Free Application for Federal Student Aid (FAFSA). This is the most important financial aid application, and it is FREE! Every student should complete the application regardless of what you think you may qualify for. We will cover the FAFSA after discussing the types of financial aid.

What are the different types of financial aid?

Grants don't have to be paid back and are need-based. The need is determined by information entered on the Free Application for Federal Student Aid (FAFSA). There are Federal and State Grants. If you demonstrated significant financial need on your FAFSA, you may be eligible for the Federal Pell Grant. If eligible for the Federal

Pell Grant, the award amount will be based on your *Expected Family Contribution (EFC)*. Availability of additional federal and state grants is determined by the college financial aid office. Factors may include need, submission date of the FAFSA, and availability of funds.

Federal Work Study (FWS) does not have to be paid back and is need-based. FWS provides part-time jobs for students, allowing the opportunity to earn money towards educational expenses. FWS encourages community service work and work related to the student's course of study. You must have a FAFSA on file in order to be considered. FWS is not guaranteed. There may be other work options available for a student aside from FWS. Check with your school's student employment office for additional options.

Scholarships don't have to be paid back and are usually merit-based. Some private third-party scholarships may be need-based, but the third-party will set their requirements, and you must apply through them. In addition to third-party scholarship awards, there are also opportunities to earn academic, athletic, institution (college/university), and department (major) scholarships. Each scholarship has its own requirements. Seek out information about scholarships to know if you meet the requirements and how to apply. Make sure you read the application carefully, fill it out completely, and meet the application DEADLINE.

Where to seek out scholarships?

- Use resources at your high school (Counselor, Library, Avid, or Upward Bound)

- Community & Religious organizations (Fraternity, Sorority, or Church)

- Consider local business or your employer

- Use your parent/guardian resources (Employer or organization membership benefits)

- Consider ethnicity-based organizations/foundations (Thurgood Marshall College Fund, NAACP etc.)

- Free Scholarship Search (Studentaid.gov/scholarships)

Loans must be paid back with interest. There are different types of education loans including federal and private loans. To become eligible for federal student loans, you must complete the FAFSA. Loan limits are based on dependency status and classification. If you are a dependent student, your parent(s) may apply for a Federal PLUS loan. Direct Subsidized Loans are the best loan option, followed by Direct Unsubsidized Loans, and, if necessary, Direct Parent PLUS Loans. (Must be enrolled in at least 6 credit-hours to be eligible for Federal Direct Loans)

Private educational loans can be obtained by applying directly with a lender such as a bank. Federal loans tend to be a better option than private loans because of the lower interest rates and more flexible payment options. In most

THE TRANSITION GUIDE & JOURNAL

cases, private loans should be the last option.

When borrowing loans, ALWAYS be aware of your loan's interest rate, repayment options, and whether you will accrue interest while enrolled. If you utilize Federal Direct Loans, be prepared to complete Entrance Counseling and sign a Master Promissory Note. Please read through the information carefully.

Additional Resources- Also, be aware of certain Exemptions and Waivers for circumstances such as Disability, Foster Care or Military that may help pay for college.

5 things you should know before starting the FAFSA:

1. You must be a U.S. citizen or an eligible noncitizen.
2. You must have a valid Social Security number.
3. Males between the ages of 18-25 must be registered with Selective Service (visit *www.sss.gov* for more information)
4. You must have a high school diploma or recognized equivalent, such as a General Educational Development (GED) certificate.
5. You must be enrolled or have plans to enroll in an eligible degree or certificate program.

The FAFSA can be completed online at fafsa.ed.gov. To electronically sign the application, you and at least one parent must first create a Federal Student Aid ID (FSA ID) The FSA ID will be utilized to confirm your identity when accessing your government financial aid information and electronically signing your federal student aid documents. (Learn more or create yours at www.fsaid.gov).

The FAFSA once opened in January but starting with the 2017-2018 application the FAFSA is now available to complete in October of each year (e.g., October 2019, for 2020-2021 award/academic year). It is imperative to check with your financial aid office or the federal student aid website for state priority submission deadlines. Most funding will be first come first served, so you want to get the FAFSA done sooner than later. If you are utilizing federal funds, you should update your FAFSA every year you plan to enroll.

Have personal and income information on hand for yourself (if applicable) and your parent(s). Using this example above, you and your family would provide income information from 2018. It should be easy to transfer the required tax information with the IRS (Internal Revenue Service) Data Retrieval Tool, which is a feature on the FAFSA. You are only excluded from entering parental information if you can answer yes to one of the dependency questions listed on the FAFSA (check www.fafsa.ed.gov). Only biological or adoptive parental information is required. If there is an unusual circumstance, contact your school financial aid office.

Completing the FAFSA doesn't assure that it is sent to your college. Be sure to add your school or school code when asked during the application. The FAFSA will only be sent to the school(s) added to the application.

Upon completion online, you should receive a Student Aid Report (SAR) within 24-48 hours. The SAR will indicate the **Expected Family Contribution (EFC)**. The EFC is a formulated number based on information reported on the FAFSA such as income and household information. The EFC is NOT the amount a family is expected to pay. The EFC has a bearing on federal pell grant eligibility and is utilized to determine *financial aid need*. Need is calculated by subtracting the EFC from the **Cost of Attendance (COA)**. The COA is the figure provided by the college/university financial office that ESTIMATES the total costs of attending that school for a period of one year. The COA components include tuition, books, travel fees, room and board, and some other school expenses.

NEED FORMULA

COST OF ATTENDANCE   -   **EFC**   =   **NEED**

_____   _____   _____

Remember this formula. It will be important each semester.

What next?

Once the FAFSA is submitted and sent to the college, you should be checking email, mail, or your college student portal. It is critical to stay in communication with your college/university to remain updated on your status.

You may be selected for verification, which could require the college financial aid office to request additional information such as tax documents or a worksheet. The purpose is to verify that the information entered on the FAFSA is accurate. The selection is random, but the college may institutionally select you if necessary. If not selected for verification, be on the lookout for an award letter. The award letter will contain the financial aid amount that is being offered by that specific school. Award letters may be different at each school.

Once you receive an award letter, compare it to your expenses. Don't include offered loans just yet. Determine the ***Direct Cost of Attendance***. Just as it is with the award letter, the COA may be different at each school. If the college has given you its ESTIMATED COA, make sure to deduct any expenses that do not apply to you. If you don't plan on living on campus, you may not need room and board. To gain a better understanding of COA, view the next Example. Create different scenarios based on the COA in the example.

EXAMPLE

ESTIMATED COST OF ATTENDANCE (COA)

Components of COA	Resident Living (On Campus)
Tuition & Fees	$15,000 full-time ($7500 per semester)
Room & Board	$5000 ($2500 per semester)
Books & Supplies	$2000
Travel/Transportation	$1500
Miscellaneous	$2000
TOTAL	$25,500 (12,750 per semester)

Why is understanding COA important?

Often, students and families see the ESTIMATED COA and make ill-advised decisions without considering or calculating the DIRECT COA, which may be significantly lower. In some cases, students prematurely borrow loans to cover estimated expenses that won't exist. As a result, some students do not return the loans funds and accrue unnecessary debt. Be mindful of your situation!! After calculating your direct COA and comparing it with your award letter, you should have an idea of your net cost (out-of-pocket cost). It is calculated by subtracting your scholarships, grants, and other financial assistance from your direct COA. The lower the net cost, the better.

Attending a College or University Out-Of-State

Most state college or universities have steep discounts for residents, and every state has a set of guidelines for establishing residency. Some states, like Utah, make it easy for non-resident students to establish residency during their freshman year. Some states make it almost impossible to gain residency as a student. Nonetheless, be sure to check the requirements for your school because residency could change your cost dramatically.

EXERCISE 7
DETERMINE FINANCIAL AID STATUS

FINANCIAL AID AWARD **VS.** **DIRECT COST OF ATTENDANCE**

(Scholarships, Grants,   **(Tuition, Housing, Meal Plan,**

Work Study + resources)   **Laundry)**

_____   _____

Determine if you have enough aid to cover your direct cost. If not, exhaust all other options before using loans. It's perfectly acceptable to contact your school's financial aid office asking for additional options. Financial aid officers are there to help students attend their school, so be courteous when corresponding with your financial aid counselor.

Explain your circumstance and anything your family might be experiencing that weren't accounted for in your FAFSA (such as change of employment). Ask if you might qualify for additional scholarships or grants. If you did not receive work-study, inquire about other on-campus jobs accepting student applicants. It won't hurt to ask questions. Hopefully, you'll find a financial aid officer that is willing to work with you.

If at that point you and/or your family do not have the resources to cover the difference (if any), it may be time to consider loan options or a different school. Make loans your LAST OPTION. If you're offered subsidized loan amount is enough to cover your projected difference, only use that loan. Use the unsubsidized loan only if necessary! The last option that the school can offer is the Federal Direct Parent Plus loan. As you make your transition, continue to position yourself to receive merit-based funding.

SATISFACTORY ACADEMIC PROGRESS (SAP)

Once you receive and utilize financial aid, you must maintain certain academic standards to remain eligible. If a student is not maintaining Satisfactory Academic Progress (SAP), financial aid will be in jeopardy. SAP is used to define academic requirements to maintain eligibility for student financial aid. Requirements vary depending on the university or college, but typically revolve around GPA, attempted hours, and completion rates.

For example:

1.   **GPA:** You may be required to maintain a grade point average of 2.0 to remain eligible for financial aid.

2.   **Completion Rate:** Your completion rate is the number of credit hours you have completed versus the number of credit hours you have attempted. If you attempt 15 credit hours and only pass 9 of the hours, you will have a 60% completion rate for that semester.

3.   **Attempted Hours:** You must complete your program with a certain number of attempted hours. If 120 credit hours are required to earn your degree, but you have attempted 130 and only completed 95, your financial aid would be in jeopardy.

Verify all SAP requirements with your college or university financial aid office.

Overall, be responsible and make well thought out decisions, because the choices you make today will impact your future. Remember, financial aid is there to help. The reality is most students, especially those from minority families, need financial aid. You must be smart about how you use it. Be sure to use all available resources such as high school counselors, financial aid counselors, and official websites.

CHAPTER ELEVEN

BUDGETING BASICS

"A budget is telling your money where to go instead of wondering where it went." -Dave Ramsey

Creating a budget is critical to your Financial Plan for several reasons including saving and more importantly making sure that you have a plan to live within your means. The basics of budget begin with Income & Expenses. Here are a few basic strategies to help you develop your budget.

INCOME WHAT IS COMING IN AND HOW OFTEN?

One of the first steps to developing a budget is determining how much income you have coming in from a job, family support, savings, financial aid, and any other streams of financial assistance. After assessing your streams of income, determine how often each stream is coming in. If you have a job, do you get paid weekly or bi-weekly?

EXPENSES WHAT IS GOING OUT AND HOW OFTEN?

he other half of your budget plan is your expenses. Tracking your expenses will help you take control of your finances and help limit stressful situations. Determine what costs you have and how often you must pay for each payment. Consider the bills you pay and purchases you make. Some of the expenses you should consider include rent, utilities, phone bill, food, gas, and subscriptions.

Fixed and Variable Expenses

Fixed expenses cost the same each time. Examples would be rent or gym memberships. A *variable expense* is one that may change. Examples include gasoline, car maintenance, or cost for books each semester.

Academic Expenses

Consider your degree plan and create a projected tuition and fee expense plan. If you are pursuing a bachelor's degree, determine your expected cost for each semester leading up to graduation.

CREATE YOUR PLAN

Now that you have gathered the necessary information become intentional! Based on the information you gathered, determine if you should create a weekly, bi-weekly, or monthly budget. If most of your expenses are generated monthly, you may want to create a monthly budget. To help with organization and structure, utilize smart device apps, spreadsheets, or start with just writing it down! Lastly, always look to adjust by cutting cost and adding streams of income.

JOURNAL NOTES

_____

_____

_____

_____

_____

_____

_____

_____

_____

_____

_____

_____

_____

_____

_____

_____

_____

_____

_____

_____

_____

_____

_____

_____

_____

_____

_____

_____

_____

_____

_____

_____

_____

_____

_____

_____

_____

_____

_____

_____

_____

_____

_____

_____

_____

_____

_____

_____

_____

_____

_____

_____

_____

_____

_____

THE TRANSITION DEGREE

Congratulations!!! You have created your college M.A.P. and earned the Transition Degree in The Law of Attraction. The purpose of the Transition program is to prepare you as current or college bound student to maximize your college experience. On the next page, you will find a temporary degree. This temporary degree will serve as a reminder that you have committed to fulfilling your degree requirements at your perspective or current college/university.

As a college student, a goal is to graduate. This step will help manifest that goal! On this degree you will be asked to fill in the following information:

- Your Name
- The Dean of your College (Department)
- The President of your College or University

It would be even better to get your Dean and President to sign it themselves! You may also cut the degree out and put it in a place where you can see it every day. Before you know it, you will have the real thing!

CLAIM YOUR DEGREE!

TRANSITION UNIVERSITY

Under authorization granted by the Transition University administration, the

Law of Attraction Degree

is hereby conferred upon

Your Name

with all Rights, Benefits, and Privileges appertaining there to in evidence of the satisfactory completion of the TU program and adherence to complete prospective or current college program.

Dean of College

University President

SUCCESS IS DUE TO

OUR STRETCHING

TO THE CHALLENGES

OF LIFE.

FAILURE COMES WHEN

WE SHRINK TO THEM.

{ -JOHN MAXWELL }

INDEX

J

L

M

N

O

P

RESOURCES

WEBSITES

GENERAL COLLEGE INFORMATION

www.CollegeBoard.org

www.BigFuture.com

www.collegeboard.org

MONEY FOR COLLEGE

www.Fafsa.ed.gov (Free Application for Federal Student Aid)

www.FastWeb.com

www.CollegeGreenLight.com

www.StudentLoans.gov

www.StudentAid.gov

www.tmcf.org

www.tomjoynerfoundation.org

COURSE TEXTBOOKS

www.Chegg.com

wwww.Amazon.com

CAREER

www.careeronestop.org

www.bls.gov

www.internships.com

www.aftercollege.com

www.volunteermatch.org

www.16personalities.com (personality test)

ADDITIONAL WEBSITE RECOMMENDATIONS

www.hardlyhome.org (Education through travel)

www.paperpencilpen.org (school supplies)

www.trailblazersinmotion.org (relationships & connections)

APPS

Chegg (rent or buy textbooks)

Amazon (textbooks and saving)

Mint (finances)

Google Calendar (scheduling & time management)

Canva (templates)

GroupMe or Slack (community/groups)

LinkedIn (business media/job search)

Indeed (job search)

BOOKS

The Secret To Success- Eric Thomas

Rich Dad Poor Dad- Robert Kiyosaki

The 48 Laws of Power- Robert Greene

Think and Grow Rich- Napoleon Hill

The Alchemist- Paulo Coelho

Students Guide To GREATNESS- Kendall Ficklin

Pass The Torch- Sterling Mark

Embrace It While You Chase It- Shaun Worthy

Her 20 SomeTHINGS- Zakiyrah Ficklin

Pushed- Raven Turner

Yes, You Can: 7 Keys to Student Success- Mike Nelson

Average To Awesome- Tim Bowers

Process- Jonathan J. Jones

POEMS

Still I Rise- Maya Angelou

Invictus- William Ernest Henley

Test of A Man- Author Unknown

If- Rudyard Kipling

DOCUMENTARIES

The Secret/The Law of Attraction

PARTNERS

THEJCSPROJECT.ORG

(Student Care Packages)

SIMPLYHELPINGFOUNDATION.ORG

(Toiletries & School Supplies)

MUKAPPAOMEGA.COM

(Sorority/Community Service)

THECOLLEGEEXPO.ORG

(HBCU College Expo)

ALSO BY PROFESSOR B

THE TRANSITION GUIDE & JOURNAL

A Simple Tool for Students to Help Maximize The College Experience

ISBN-13: 978-1535337250
ISBN-10: 1535337257

THE TRANSITION

A SIMPLE GUIDE TO HELP VISIONARIES TRANSITION TO THE NEXT LEVEL

ISBN-13: 978-1540791191
ISBN-10: 154079119X

2nd Edition
THE TRANSITION GUIDE & JOURNAL

A Simple Tool for Students to Help Maximize The College Experience

ISBN-13: 978-1973955092
ISBN-10: 1973955091

CONNECT WITH PROFESSOR B ON SOCIAL MEDIA

@BLAKEMOTIVATES

BLAKEMOTIVATES

TAG PROFESOR B & HASHTAG

#MOVINGHOPE #BLAKEMOTIVATES
#THETRANSITIONBOOK #TRANSITIONU #PROFESSORB

Would you like to book Professor B for your next event? If so, contact us via email at info@blakemotivates.com or via phone at 713-584-0770. You may also visit www.blakemotivates.com

Made in the USA
Columbia, SC
20 June 2021

40419651R00085